Making Silent Stones Sing

a chapbook of poems

by

Susan Cummins Miller

Finishing Line Press
Georgetown, Kentucky

Making Silent Stones Sing

a chapbook of poems

Copyright © 2022 by Susan Cummins Miller
ISBN 978-1-64662-755-4 First Edition
All rights reserved under International and Pan-American Copyright Conventions. No part of this book may be reproduced in any manner whatsoever without written permission from the publisher, except in the case of brief quotations embodied in critical articles and reviews.

ACKNOWLEDGMENTS

I am grateful to the editors of the following publications in which the listed poems originally appeared, some in slightly different form:

Impermanent Earth: "On Reading a Poem by Ghalib during the Pandemic"
Iris Literary Journal: "Renewal at Djerassi"
More Voices of New Mexico anthology (Rio Grande Books): "Unharvested Water"
OASIS Journal: "Genesis" and "Spider Woman"
Roundup! Western Writers of America Presents Great Stories of the West from Today's Leading Western Writers anthology (La Frontera Publishing): "Two Roads Diverged"
Sandcutters 2012 Contest Winners' Anthology (Arizona State Poetry Society): "Entering the Mojave"
Unstrung: "Fire on Friday"
What Wildness Is This: Women Write about the Southwest anthology (The University of Texas Press): "The Bone-Man's Apprentice"
Without a Doubt: poems on faith anthology (*New York Quarterly*): "The Way that Lies between"
The Write Launch: "Making Silent Stones Sing" and "Cracking the Code"

Publisher: Leah Huete de Maines
Editor: Christen Kincaid
Cover Art: Susan Cummins Miller
Author Photo: Susan Cummins Miller
Cover Design: Elizabeth Maines McCleavy

Order online: www.finishinglinepress.com
also available on amazon.com

Author inquiries and mail orders:
Finishing Line Press
PO Box 1626
Georgetown, Kentucky 40324
USA

Table of Contents

1. Deep time, Grand Canyon 1

The Bone-Man's Apprentice 2

No Roof but Sky: Roberts Mountains, Nevada 3

That Summer Visit to Newport Beach 5

Genesis 6

Fire on Friday 7

Two Roads Diverged 8

Unharvested Water 10

The Unexpected Guest 11

Deep Time 12

2. This one existence 13

The Way that Lies between 14

Entering the Mojave 15

Splitting Shale in the Marble Mountains 17

Making Silent Stones Sing 18

Renewal at Djerassi 20

Cracking the Code 21

On Reading a Poem by Ghalib during the Pandemic 23

Spider Woman 24

The Power of a Word 25

*For Jonathan, Jordan, and Logan, and
in memory of my parents and Steve Kowit*

1.

Deep time, Grand Canyon:
From rafting geologists
soft cries of wonder.

The Bone-Man's Apprentice

Between Route 66
and the Old Spanish Trail
we hiked serrated ridges, discovering
a cache of fossil bones preserved
on a limy sandstone ledge
in the heart of the Mojave.

Under your watchful eye
I chiseled away the barren, protective strata,
exposing teeth and dimpled bone—a horse's skull
no longer than my hand, concealed
for eighteen million years. With clear drops
of Glyptol, I sealed the fragile fragments.

You showed me how to swaddle the delicate palate
in layers of TP, how to mix the Plaster of Paris.
I poured tepid canteen water into the dented basin, added
pale-gray powder that smelled like kindergarten, warmed
numb fingers in the exothermic reaction, dipped strips
of rough brown burlap in the thick white soup.

Laughing, we smoothed the gooey paste
on fossil and rock pedestal, our fingers
and forearms taking on the virginal hue until
neither of us could identify
where our bodies ended
and the sun-bleached hills began.

No Roof but Sky: Roberts Mountains, Nevada

Sitting alone on a rough boulder
of Lone Mountain Dolomite at the place
where Willow Creek leaves the confines
of the canyon to meander over the unsorted surface
of an old alluvial fan. Shorts reveal
sun-browned legs. Feet that trudged miles
since daybreak recover in the cold, rippling water
of the creek. Beneath my stone throne
and a covering of valley fill lies a range-bounding
normal fault. Cottonwood leaves flutter
and whisper in the breeze schussing down
the canyon. The valley spreads out—
not a vehicle, dwelling or rancher in sight
from here to the next range over. Wild mustangs
stream like a wavering banner
across distant foothills, aiming for a waterhole.
Dust devils dance in their wake. The nearby corral
is empty again after yesterday's round up, but still
I hear the bawling of neutered, branded calves,
the frantic bleating of cows; still I see a boy of 8 or 9
carrying a handful of Rocky Mountain oysters,
popping them, one by one, in his mouth
in a rite of passage
akin to the reason I am here, now,
mapping Paleozoic rocks laid down when life
was confined to the seas, when some fish wore boney
exoskeletons, when trilobites hoovered debris
from the seafloor like horseshoe crabs
off today's Atlantic coast. In the field camp HQ,
a farmhouse abandoned for better digs
at least forty years ago, pans clatter
on the elderly propane stove. In the center
of the compound one of the cooking team starts
the evening fire in a circle of blackened stones,
covering it with the grill. Pork chops tonight.

Two students argue over how much water
to add to the lemonade and ice tea mixes
in mismatched Coleman jugs. Fingers strum
guitar strings. A harmonica searches
for the right key—finds it, eventually, as the clouds turn
salmon, crimson, and gold. Baritone and tenor voices
pick up the melody of a song about country roads
and going home. Someone whistles harmony.
The only other female is taking a shower with
sun-warmed water in a makeshift structure the shape
of Doctor Who's phone booth. Absent door
and curtains, the three-sided box offers
unobstructed views of the endless, sage-covered,
reassuringly empty basin. The indigo sky lowers,
enveloping canyon first, then valley. Alpenglow
lingers on distant peaks. A mate calls
my name, the yodel muted by gurgling creek,
by camp noise, by music and the rising wind.
I don't answer, convinced that there will never be
another sunset as ripe, another moment
as private and pure, another song sung
by companions as copacetic as these. It is enough
to make a hardened geologist weep.

That Summer Visit to Newport Beach
For T. G. M.

The palm reader, wearing a varicolored turban
        and flowing robes, stubs out
        a cigarillo and picks up
        my friend's right hand, tracing
        the palm lines, making pronouncements.

The head line slashes a diagonal
        across his palm, resolute and unwavering
        as the path of a coyote
        under a full moon.

The love line is single, deep, straight
        and as purple as his favorite song,
        but his success line branches
        like a birch tree—discontinuous,
        one branch replacing another.

The reader searches
        for a heart line. Gives up
        with a frown and moves on.

The lifeline curves
        then stops abruptly. Or does it?
        Perhaps those small transverse segments
        are like faults connecting short strands
        of the San Andreas—suggesting breakage,
        new tracks, renaissance.

We leave, laughing,
        no wiser than before.
        But twenty-one years later, on a Tuesday
        in May, a gunshot stops
        the beating of his heart.

Genesis

Remember when we climbed that limestone tor
out in Nevada? Craving privacy
and summer-hardened bodies we spread your
chambray work shirt under aging pine trees
to shield our naked skin from needles, twigs
and time-etched talus. Afterwards, your head
soft-pillowed on my thigh, we shared ripe figs,
red apples, water—canteen-warm—and bread.
We stared at skies where falcons flew. You tried
to speak—a croak. I brushed ants from my boot.
"This doesn't mean I'll marry you," you cried,
then shied from me and bit into the fruit.
The silence grew about us, hot and still.
We lobbed half-eaten apples down the hill.

Fire on Friday

When night falls
in sheltered canyon, dizzying
landscape of alcoves, cliffs
and caves, trapped on a ledge
the vertical swallows us.
Below, calm waters hide
rippling crosscurrents.
No going back.
Not tonight.

We merge with the deep, flowing
darkness and clicking consonants
of bighorn sheep stepping daintily
down to the river. Sudden constellations
of eerie red glows resolve into headlamps
like light-shifts of stars
moving away
in time, in space.

Ceremony
provides perspective: Fire
on Friday from fiddlehead
tinder. Cedar-bark tea in a rock-
slab kitchen. Entrapped evolves
into enchanted. Sip.
Close down.
Let go.

Two Roads Diverged

Dodging raindrops and lightning bolts
I ducked into the split-log bar
in Montello. Bud Country, but Dave
rustled up a warm Guinness
from the back.

My brown hair was long then, twisted
up off my neck and secured
with a piece of leather
and a wooden pick, sharpened
at both ends.

Played pool with three geologists
and a cowboy—just a way to pass the time,
a way to drive the geologic puzzles
from my mind so I could sleep. Lost,
on both counts.

Walking back to the motel
in the sultry darkness, under restless stars,
the Leach Mountains at my back
the valley stretching east forever—
or to Utah,

whichever came first—I passed
that cowboy, smoking behind the store.
He tossed out a proposition
like a half-smoked Camel.
Unfiltered.

The wind riffled the cottonwood leaves.
Black shadows played tag. A killdeer piped
from the sage-covered slope.
A horned owl answered.
Awkwardly,

laughing, I turned on my heel,
grinding the metaphorical butt
into the muddy road. Yet,
thirty years later, I'm still
wondering.

Unharvested Water

Gila Wilderness, 6 p.m.
Thunder's an oak barrel rolling
down cliffs, drawing me into
the storm. Buffeting wind. Mist
on bare skin. Quicksilver cloud-surge
on ancient caldera.

Raindrops thrum differently
on tin roofs, trailer shells
and faded canvas tents.
This Tuesday evening
drops sizzle like burgers
on that roadside grill
in Oasis, Nevada.
Maybe if I hadn't stopped there
on the way back from town
I'd have caught you
before you struck camp. Maybe.
But would it have changed things?

Unharvested water
courses down trails, ponds
in the low places, seeps
between sand grains
displacing stale air,
collecting like old regrets,
in the starless, secret places
where no one
can pitch a tent.

The Unexpected Guest

Sometimes in August
the wild monsoon winds blow through
carrying scents from the Gulf of Mexico,
the Sierra Madre and all points
in between. Once, in the Chiricahuas,
one such storm delivered a pelican
to the peak of the portico, where
he perched, apparently confused
by foreign smells and sights and the lack
of water, water, anywhere—alone,
like me, but unable to recognize
the yearning for other.

Below him: the solidity
of concrete deck, rock wall. Above:
endless, empty blue. Patiently, he smoothed
wayward feathers back into order
with ungainly skill, then dozed through
the humid heat of afternoon like an old monk
in an abbey garden. At nightfall his dark form,
a silhouette against the lighter sky, shrugged
and flexed broad wings. Turning beak
into the breeze he launched himself
up and out, pulled eastward
by star-guides and the rising gibbous
moon. When he disappeared,
even the shifting shadows
seemed blacker, emptier.

Deep Time

This vigil in our small orbits turning,
turning through the singing
and the silence, this buttery-smooth slice
of moment, this journey: All signs leading
like the bent-finger-curve of two-track
out to the farthest horizon, never returning.
Forgotten. Remembered. Reborn.

Tell me we lived with purpose, eyes
bristling and flickering in the elliptic
light of day. And later, our breath besieging
the stone rings of sound as we hiked
the darkening trail, remember
how the wind picked up, the crickets sang
and then stopped

when the western diamondback, scales
aglow, struck the forked branch
I swung before me at ground level
to hold danger at bay? Remember
how we danced—and did not dance—
by the Diamond Valley springs
that hot July night?

2.

This one existence:
pale-gray wisp of cloud drifting
past the full-blown moon.

The Way that Lies between

Take time
to lie fallow. Withdraw
into landscape and symbol. Walk
the hills, quiet your mind, absorb

the contours of the earth, the meter
in your steps. Hear the crunch
of rock and gravel, the whisper
of sand. Hear your spirit chant

silently, fervently. Listen
to the cactus wren, to mourning
doves and curve-billed thrashers singing up
the sun. Listen to horned owls call

and the squeaks of pipistrelles winging
in the moonlight. Listen, walk, until breath
and step rhyme, until mind
and heartbeat merge,

until even that subtle music
fades away—and all that remains
is the way that lies between
inhale   and exhale.

Entering the Mojave

Where ancient seas
once split a continent, asphalt highways link
a far-flung people. With shuttered eyes
the hordes pass through.

This ruptured crust,
this dry land, drowning in its own debris,
is far too hot, too cold, inhospitable,
too barren, thorny, inconsiderate.

Here, we cannot hide
in the shadows of tall oaks and poplars,
our voices are not muffled by the rush of water
over stones.

We who stop
must face our scars
from wounds incised like petroglyphs
on wrinkled skin of upthrust rock.

Or turn away,
to lose ourselves in cities
where neon lights obscure and shadows reveal
half-truths and obsequies.

And yet, this land
of hoodoos and phantom lakes bewitches,
promising a solitude
more precious than rain.

So I escape
into empty canyons, climb
the desert-varnished ledges, bare my head
to unsheltering sky.

I draw deep
the untainted air, let the unrelenting sun
suck poison from my soul,
let pain melt

into mirage,
set my dreams adrift
on thermals, watch them rise
to mingle with the stars.

Splitting Shale in the Marble Mountains

I found I could not search
my soul till I recovered
long-lost shards and reassembled
the mirror. Jagged holes
marked missing slivers. Yet,
through those spaces something shimmers,
delicate as sea lilies, translucent
as the dawn. Perhaps used souls

are meant to break,
to be sloughed off
as they're outgrown, collecting
like scraps of carapace
on ancient Cambrian sands.
Perhaps this layered black hash
of trilobite debris—
wave-winnowed, compressed,

lithified and uplifted
in the desolate middle of the Mojave—
is just a jumble of soul-bits and -pieces
shed eons ago, releasing
a new soul, free and whole,
to swim saline currents
warm as vein-blood.

Making Silent Stones Sing

i.

Picture Rocks Canyon: Paisley
scarlet bandana caught on gray thornbush
sprouting from naked rock. Lavender-
blooming ironwood, swift
zebra-tailed lizards, and always
the cactus wrens for company.

ii.

If you sit
where basalt layers first enter
the canyon, clear your mind, focus
on nothing, you'll discover
a faint figure pecked
in black patina: Elongated
body, arms upraised, feet planted firmly
on nothing
but groundmass. Nearby,

inscribed on
other smooth outcrops, circles
and loops, squares and rectangles: Messages left
by archaic writers. How many hundred times
have you trudged by
without stopping, intent
on completing the loop trail—a metaphorical
circle beginning and ending
in your room?

iii.

Note to self: If it is the journey
that matters and not
the arbitrary destination, then remember
the magic in this impromptu stop.
And before you leave, place your hand
on the petroglyphs, acknowledge
the spark leaping artist to artist and making
silent stones sing.

Renewal at Djerassi

Tuesday's a triple-banana-slug kind of day:
One at the tomb-dark entrance
to *Estaciones de Luz*. Two in the creek's
muddy islands, built on basalt.

Spiders spin webs across
my twilight path. A school of polliwogs wriggles
in a steel tank that once watered cattle. California
buttercups, an aging trillium, and a stalk
of miniature lupine hide in a poppy field. While within

the Stations of Light's curving maze-like,
womb-like walls, where marble steps direct my boots
first up, then downward, a light beam catches
a three-leafed lady fern unfurling.

Cracking the Code

i.

Starting out, hard pavement consumes
wishes and hopes—polarizes, compresses
emotion: Too little time to make space

for us. Too little time
to make changes. The burning
tragedy of too little time.

ii.

Itinerant workers prune
our old willow, revealing boles bending

in opposite directions: north toward
the mountains, south toward the light.

iii.

The gardener pontificates,
arms waving. One plant thrives. Another
dies. It's all about

roots: shoving between pebbles, cobbles,
boulders and sand, poking, prying, reaching, gripping,
sucking moisture, thrusting caliche aside, leaching

precious nutrients from clay and rock. Interstices
yield wiggle room—tiny hairs, sensitive
as mole whiskers, send coded messages to probing

root tip and anchor elegant saguaro standing, arms uplifted
to sun and stars, to air and rain, tomorrow
and today—unflinching. It's about roots.

iv.

I lock the door on the double-dreaming
past, on flashy simplicity, aloof
contemporary fare, temporary decor damnably
full of faux everything—

a single row of pictures and understated
wallpaper in a sky-lit room, subliminally
pandering to the adolescent sexuality
in time-worn allegories. Locking the door's

a grassroots movement that leaves
no trace. Action creates obvious uneasiness,
but who doesn't love the raw power, the erotic
asymmetry of starting over?

On Reading a Poem by Ghalib during the Pandemic

Your world of infinite possibilities contracts
during "voluntary" confinement. Yet
even the smallest prison cell
contains enough space
for a single
step.

Spider Woman

The spider spins
a single strand of red that floats
on desert winds whistling
through the succulents.

She does not think:
*How difficult it is to weave
a web on windy days.*

She simply climbs
that yucca leaf, lets go,
and trusts the anchor,
trusts the wind.

The Power of a Word

The pool is still.
No ripples slide down curved
blue-plaster walls.

But then,
the pump comes on, trapped
air gushes through idle jets, a million ripples instantly
collide, refracting sunlight. Waves split
and merge, weaving a tapestry
of intersecting lines.

Just so,
does one spoken word, one
exhaled sound, charge
the air and transform
the world.

Tucson writer **Susan Cummins Miller**, a research affiliate of the University of Arizona's Southwest Institute for Research on Women, holds degrees in anthropology, history, and geology, with a focus on vertebrate paleontology and stratigraphy. She worked as a field geologist and taught geology and oceanography before turning to writing fiction, nonfiction, and poetry. She has been writer-in-residence at the Djerassi Resident Artists Program, Woodside, CA and the Pima County Public Library, Tucson, AZ.

Miller is the author of the novels *Death Assemblage, Detachment Fault, Quarry, Hoodoo, Fracture,* and *Chasm,* four of which were finalists for the WILLA Award in contemporary fiction. She compiled and edited *A Sweet, Separate Intimacy: women writers of the American frontier, 1800-1922,* a finalist for the Longan Award, and received the Tucson Poetry Festival's Will Inman Award. Her poetry, essays, and short fiction have appeared in, or are forthcoming in, numerous journals and anthologies, including *What Wildness Is This: Women Write about the Southwest; Global Warming; So West: So Deadly; New York Quarterly's Without a Doubt: poems illustrating faith;* and *What We Talk about When We Talk about It: variations on the theme of love* I, II. A book of poems, *Deciphering the Desert,* is forthcoming from Finishing Line Press.

www.ingramcontent.com/pod-product-compliance
Lightning Source LLC
LaVergne TN
LVHW040118080426
835507LV00041B/1614